# DIARY
# OF A
# MARINE
# BIOLOGIST

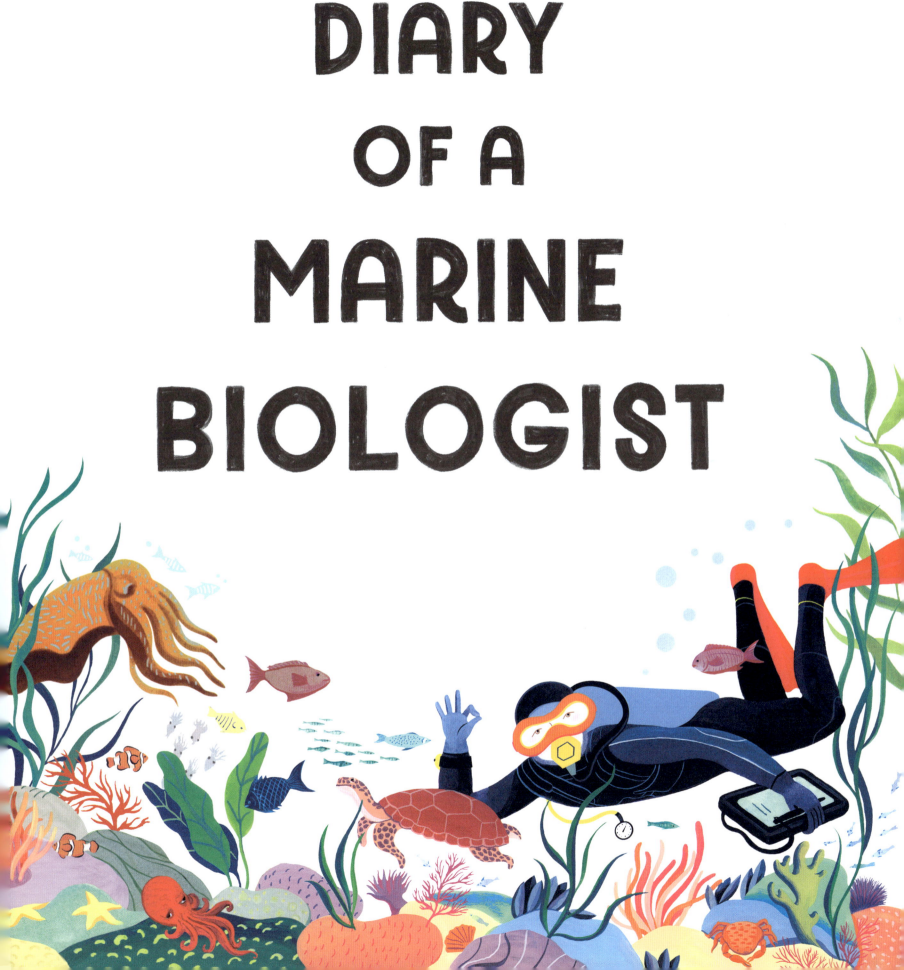

*To Banksia and all those working
to protect our oceans — A.T.*

*To Ivy — S.W.*

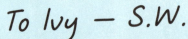

*Diary of a Marine Biologist*
Walker Books Australia Pty Ltd
Gadigal and Wangal Country
Locked Bag 22, Newtown
NSW 2042 Australia
www.walkerbooks.com.au

Walker Books Australia acknowledges the Traditional Owners of the country on which we work, the Gadigal and Wangal peoples of the Eora Nation, and recognizes their continuing connection to the land, waters and culture. We pay our respect to their Elders past and present.

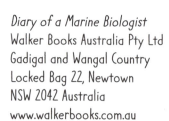

A catalogue record for this book is available from the National Library of Australia

ISBN: 978 1 761602 53 5

Book design by Sarah Mitchell
The illustrations for this book were created by hand, using gouache and inks.
The scientific illustrations were created digitally.
Printed and bound in China

EU Authorized Representative: HackettFlynn Ltd.,
36 Cloch Choirneal, Balrothery, Co. Dublin, K32 C942, Ireland.
EU@walkerpublishinggroup.com

10 9 8 7 6 5 4 3 2 1

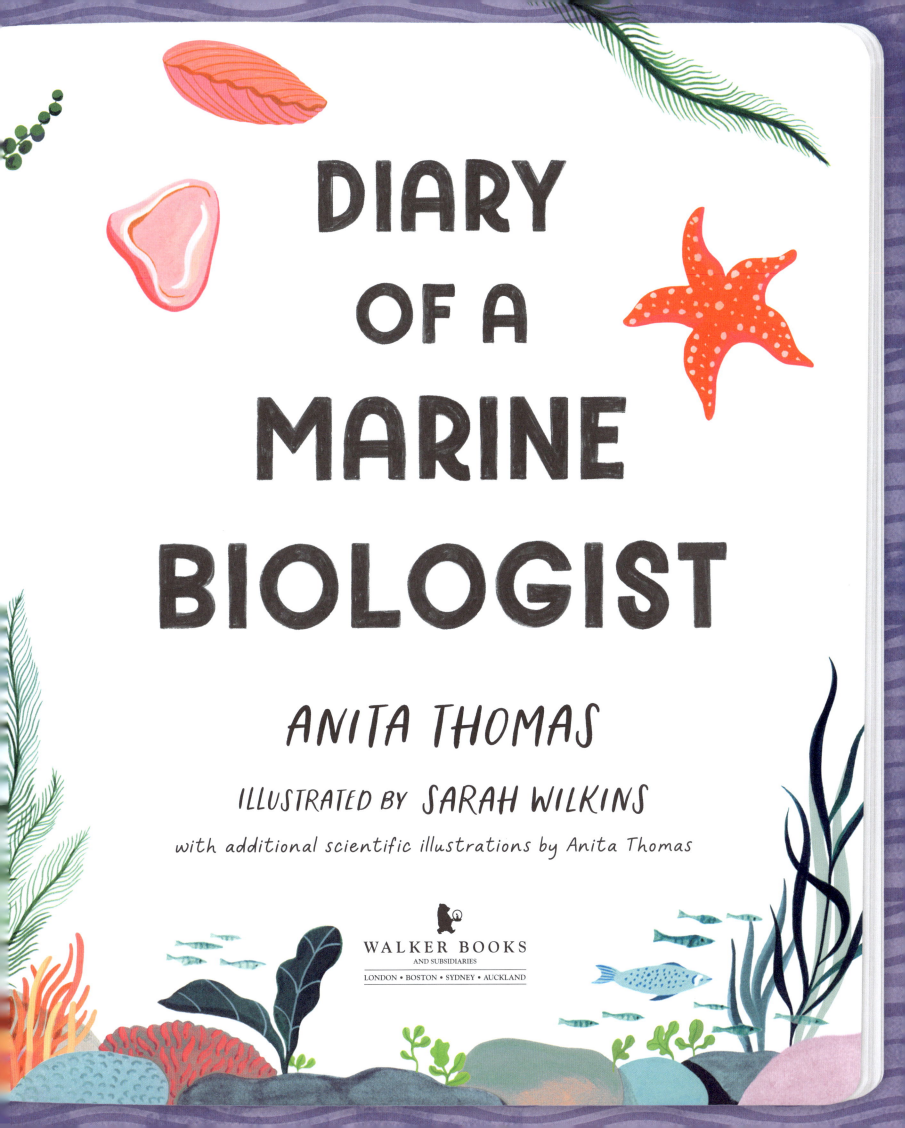

# DIARY
# OF A
# MARINE
# BIOLOGIST

## ANITA THOMAS

### ILLUSTRATED BY SARAH WILKINS

with additional scientific illustrations by Anita Thomas

WALKER BOOKS

AND SUBSIDIARIES

LONDON • BOSTON • SYDNEY • AUCKLAND

# MONDAY
## PLANNING THE WEEK

TIME: _8:00 am_

WEATHER: _17°C Cloudy_

LOCATION: _My office_

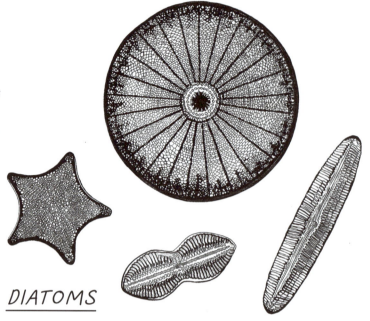

DIATOMS

Hi there! I'm Emma, and I study all the amazing creatures that live in the ocean. I've measured **sea turtles** at the Great Barrier Reef and counted baby turtles as they hatched out of their eggs. In West Papua, I once attached a little backpack with a tiny computer inside, called a tag, to a **whale shark** to help keep track of where it swam.

This week, I have some cool adventures planned. I'll be tracking down **whales** to hear them sing, taking care of **baby clownfish** to help protect them, watching how clever **cuttlefish** behave, going underwater with scuba gear to visit a special reef where **oysters** are coming back to life, and even looking for mysterious **sea snakes**. It's going to be a super exciting week exploring the ocean.

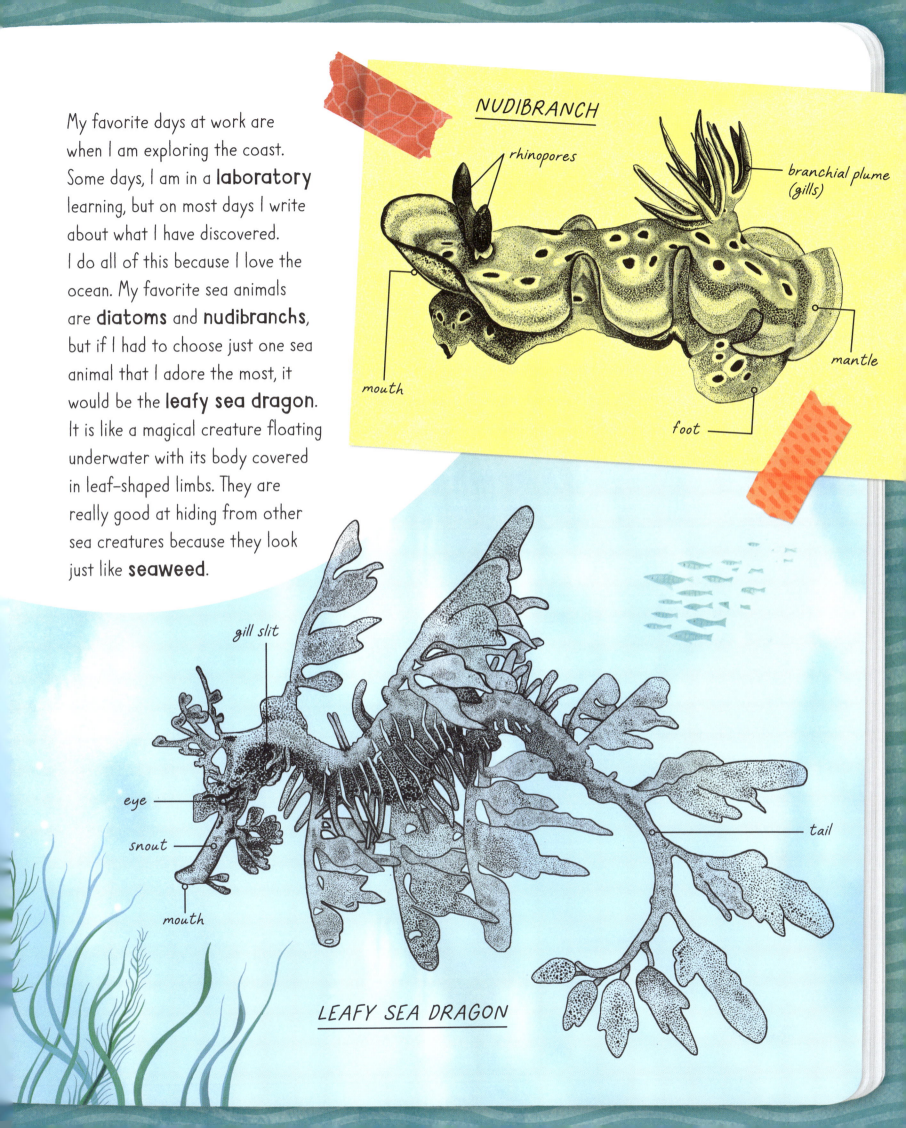

My favorite days at work are when I am exploring the coast. Some days, I am in a **laboratory** learning, but on most days I write about what I have discovered. I do all of this because I love the ocean. My favorite sea animals are **diatoms** and **nudibranchs**, but if I had to choose just one sea animal that I adore the most, it would be the **leafy sea dragon**. It is like a magical creature floating underwater with its body covered in leaf-shaped limbs. They are really good at hiding from other sea creatures because they look just like **seaweed**.

## NUDIBRANCH

rhinopores

branchial plume (gills)

mantle

foot

mouth

## LEAFY SEA DRAGON

gill slit

eye

snout

mouth

tail

# OCEAN FACTS

**1**

70% of the planet is ocean.

**2**

Less than 10% of oceans have been explored by humans.

**3**

Over 50% of the earth's oxygen comes from the ocean.

**4**

A global temperature rise of 2°C would eliminate 99% of today's coral reefs.

**5**

There are up to 14 million tons of microplastics in the sea — the equivalent of dumping two rubbish trucks into the ocean per minute.

**6**

The ocean tastes salty because just like the salt that we eat, it contains sodium chloride. The salts arrive in the sea from dissolved minerals from rocks on land.

# SCHEDULE:

MONDAY - 8 am Planning the week

TUESDAY - 5 am Whale surveys

WEDNESDAY - 9 am Clownfish nursery

THURSDAY - 11 am Diving with giant cuttlefish

FRIDAY - 9 am Searching for sea snakes

SATURDAY - 8 am Monitoring a restored oyster reef

SUNDAY - 7 am Surfing with Jessica

This week is full of activities, so I better make a list of everything I will need...

# CHECKLIST

- Notebook and pen
- Binoculars
- Camera
- Raincoat
- Hydrophone
- Scuba diving gear
- Quadrats
- Measuring tape
- Surfboard

# TUESDAY
## WHALE MONITORING

TIME: _5:00 am_

WEATHER: _13°C Rainy_

LOCATION: _Fowlers Bay_

Today I went on a two-hour boat trip to find **whales**. When I felt a bit seasick in the big waves, I remembered a trick to feel better and looked at the flat land far away on the horizon. We spotted the whales as they were blowing water out of their **blowholes** with a big whoosh! sound. We moved toward them very slowly and before we knew it, we were surrounded by a pod of Southern Right Whales and their cute newborn **calves**.

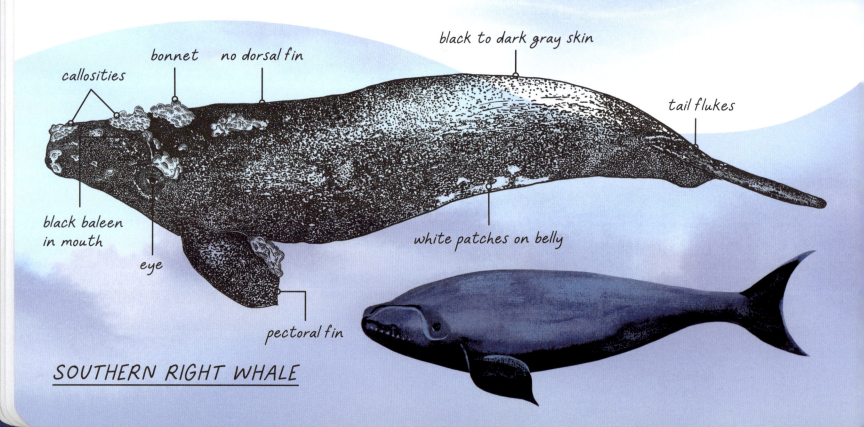

callosities

bonnet

no dorsal fin

black to dark gray skin

tail flukes

black baleen in mouth

eye

pectoral fin

white patches on belly

SOUTHERN RIGHT WHALE

We stopped the boat's engine and lowered a special microphone called a **hydrophone** into the water. I could hear the whales talking to each other. Their songs sounded like underwater **trumpets**, and I even heard sounds that were like **belches**, **moans**, **rumbles**, **growls** and **gunshots**. We recorded all these different sounds and sorted them into groups that were similar. I wonder what the whales are saying.

pattern of callosities on southern right whale

TOP VIEW

Today I also photographed 15 adults and 6 calves and recorded the number, shape, and position of the **callosities** on their head. Their callosity patterns are as unique to whales as fingerprints are to humans.

Many whales return to this coastline each year between May and October to have their babies.

In the past, whales were hunted until they almost disappeared. Thankfully, hunting them is not allowed anymore. Now, **counting** how many whales and calves come back to this place helps us to know if their group is getting bigger or smaller. The good news is their numbers are slowly increasing. We will share what we have found so that the **government** can make better plans to **protect** the whales.

It was late when we got back to the boat ramp. On my way home, I could not stop thinking about how lucky I was to have spent time with these enormous, gentle giants.

# SOUTHERN RIGHT WHALE FACTS

GLOBAL CONSERVATION STATUS: LEAST CONCERN
SCIENTIFIC NAME: EUBALAENA AUSTRALIS
SIZE: 59 FEET

**1** They are baleen whales, or toothless whales, that have baleen plates in their mouths similar to bristles that are used to sieve tiny creatures from the water.

**2** Their name comes from whalers, who thought they were the 'right' whale to hunt because they swam close to shore, floated when dead, and produced a large amount of oil when harvested.

**3** Sound waves travel faster and louder underwater than on land, so scientists believe that some whales can hear each other from 1000 miles away – that's like a long-distance call from Australia to New York.

**4** Whale poop is important for climate change. It contains iron, a trace element that single-celled plants called phytoplankton use for **photosynthesis**.

**5** Whales eat tiny crustaceans such as krill, amphipods, and copepods.

**6** A calf weighs 1.5 tons, which is equal to the weight of a car.

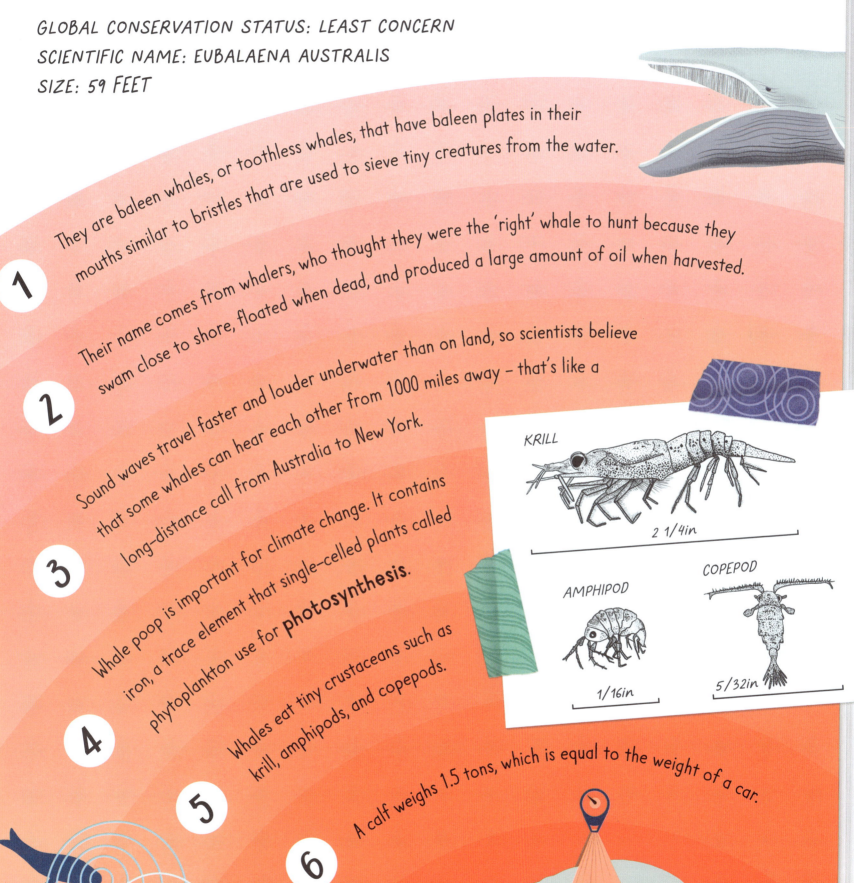

KRILL
2 1/4in

AMPHIPOD
1/16in

COPEPOD
5/32in

# WEDNESDAY
## SAVING NEMO

TIME: _9:00 am_

WEATHER: _11°C Stormy_

LOCATION: _Clownfish hatchery_

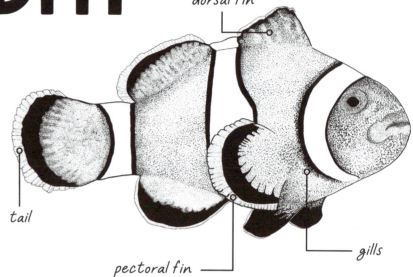

dorsal fin

tail

pectoral fin

gills

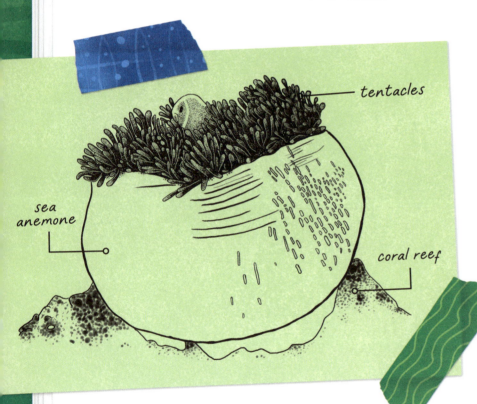

tentacles

sea anemone

coral reef

Exciting news! More baby **clownfish** hatched overnight. The mom and dad clownfish had been cleaning the clay pot in their tank for days. Normally, in the wild, clownfish lay their eggs near a protective, venomous **anemone**, but in our nursery, a pot works just as well.

Last week, the mom clownfish laid eggs, and since then she has been **guarding** them while the dad takes care of the eggs. He spends the day **cleaning** and **fanning** them with his fins to keep them fresh and full of **oxygen**.

The largest clownfish in a pair is always the mom and she is in charge and very protective. When I clean her tank, she bites my hand if it gets too close to her eggs. I counted a thousand eggs on her clay pot yesterday. I could tell they were about to hatch because I saw lots of tiny **silver and black eyes** looking up at me.

My first task today was to transfer the baby clownfish, called **fry**, to a new tank so that the adults cannot eat them. I set up the fry tank with **seawater**, an **air stone**, a **heater**, a **thermometer**, and lots of **food**.

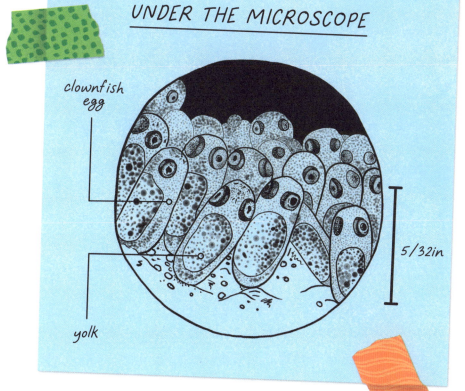

## UNDER THE MICROSCOPE

clownfish egg

yolk

5/32in

While they were in their eggs, the clownfish **embryos** used the **yolk** for energy, but now that they have hatched, the fry are hungry. Today, I gave them tiny live **rotifers** to eat.

The captive-bred clownfish born in our nursery are important for **CONSERVATION**. Once they grow bigger and stronger, we can sell them to pet stores.

In the past, millions of clownfish were taken from the wild every year for **home aquariums**. They were so popular they disappeared. But things have changed thanks to **breeding programs** like ours. Sadly, most marine fish pets are still caught in the wild. It is important for us to learn how other marine fish and creatures breed so that we can raise them in a **nursery** too.

After setting up the tank and moving the fry to safety, I packed the car, threw in my scuba diving gear, and drove to where the **giant cuttlefish** live.

# CLOWNFISH FACTS

GLOBAL CONSERVATION STATUS: LEAST CONCERN
SCIENTIFIC NAME: AMPHIPRION PERCULA
SIZE: 4 1/4 INCHES

**1** Clownfish live on average for 10 years. Scientists estimate their age from counting growth rings on their ear bones, called otiliths, just like tree trunks.

**2** Just like corals, anemones bleach from global warming, making clownfish vulnerable to extinction from climate change.

**3** They live in groups of unrelated clownfish in symbiotic anemones on coral reefs.

**4** Clownfish eggs hatch in about 7 to 10 days.

**5** There are 28 different species of clownfish.

# THURSDAY

## DANCING WITH CUTTLEFISH

TIME: _11:00 am_

WEATHER: _23°C Sunny_

LOCATION: _Whyalla_

I put my scuba diving gear on and walked to the rocky shore with my dive buddy, Simon. We did a safety check to make sure we both had our **oxygen tanks**, **buoyancy vests**, **regulators**, **weight belts**, **masks**, and **fins** before heading into the chilly water together.

Swimming with **giant cuttlefish** is like being at an underwater disco. The special **cells** in their skin, called **chromatophores**, flash and flicker like colorful neon lights. They do not pay much attention to us as we glide by. All they care about is finding a **mate**.

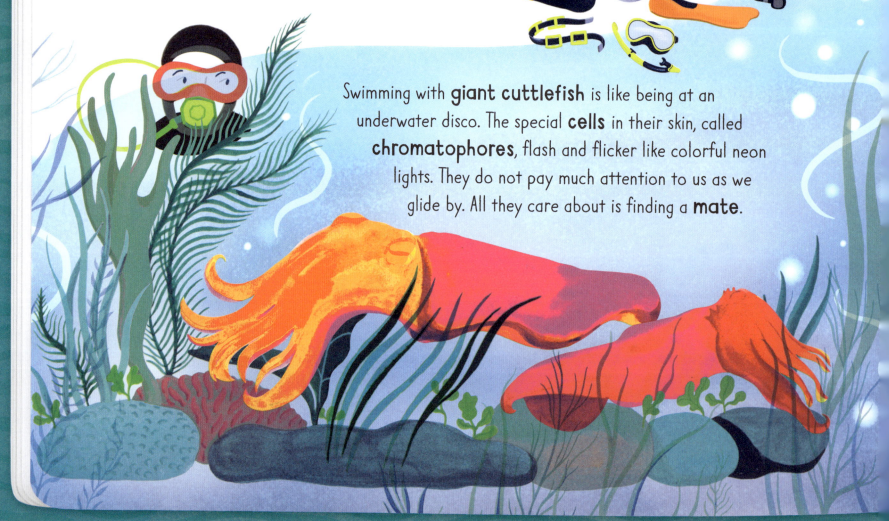

Cuttlefish are **chameleons** of the sea. I watched how they quickly change the patterns and color of their skin to hide and **communicate**. I shadowed some cuttlefish and documented every activity: when they rested, fought, mated, or flirted. I also captured videos of boy cuttlefish flashing vibrant **colors** and **patterns** to woo the girls and then quickly changing to blend back in with the seaweed.

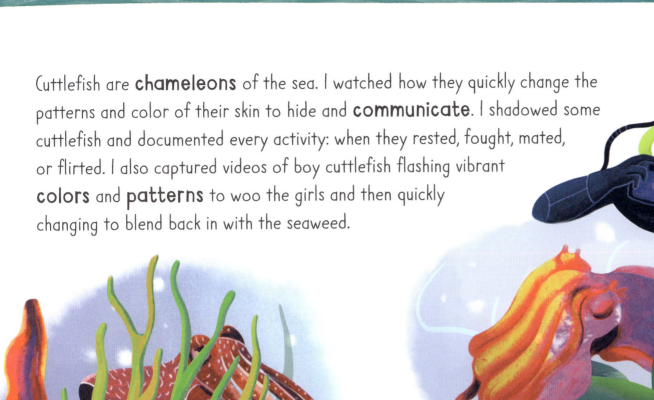

Being big and appearing strong makes the girl cuttlefish interested. But the smaller boys have to be **clever** to get noticed. We saw them using a trick to fool others by changing how they look to seem like a girl cuttlefish. This way, they avoid fighting with a bigger male and can safely get close to a girl to become friends and maybe start a **family**. I think that's really smart.

## CUTTLEFISH

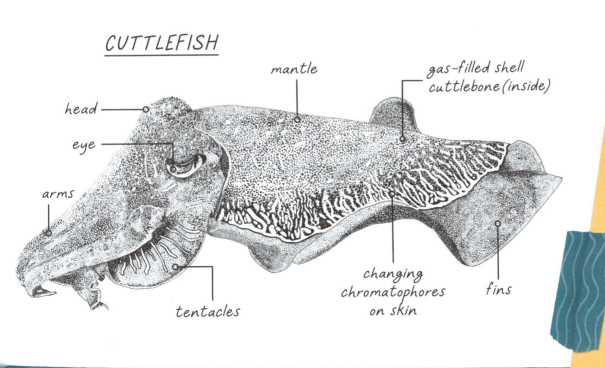

head

eye

arms

mantle

gas-filled shell
cuttlebone (inside)

tentacles

changing
chromatophores
on skin

fins

## CUTTLEBONE

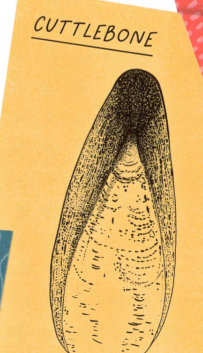

MARINE PROTECTED AREA

Watching how cuttlefish behave helps scientists learn about their lives and how to keep them **safe**. Most of the time, giant cuttlefish live by themselves, but every winter, something incredible happens. Up to **200,000 cuttlefish** gather here, and this is the only place in the world where this happens. That is why this coastline is a special place called a **marine sanctuary**. It is like a safe zone in the ocean where no plants or animals can be taken away, so cuttlefish can live peacefully.

While I rinsed my scuba equipment with fresh water and hung it up to dry, my mind wandered to tomorrow ... when I will be in the museum's **sea snake** lab.

# CUTTLEFISH FACTS

GLOBAL CONSERVATION STATUS: NEAR THREATENED
SCIENTIFIC NAME: SEPIA APAMA
SIZE: UP TO 3 FEET

**1**

Cuttlefish are gentle creatures
but can eject black ink and bite with
their powerful beak if threatened.

**2**

Cuttlefish are not fish;
they are more like relatives
of octopuses or squids.

**3**

Giant cuttlefish are the largest cuttlefish
in the world but they're not as big as the
colossal squid (46 feet) that lives
in the deepest parts of the sea.

# FRIDAY
## SEARCHING FOR SEA SNAKES

TIME: _9:00 am_

WEATHER: _16°C Rainy_

LOCATION: _Museum Laboratory_

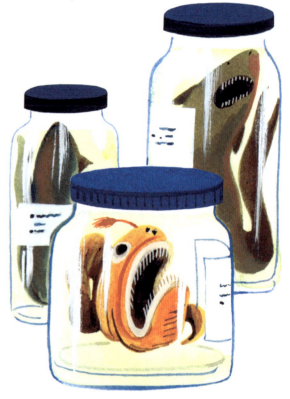

The museum **laboratories** have rooms full of jars with weird and rare animals like Colossal Squid, Cookie Cutter Sharks, and Anglerfish preserved in **ethanol**.

I was at the museum on a detective's mission trying to identify a **tropical sea snake** we had found on a field survey.

We had spent two weeks on a boat, swimming in **seagrass** beds and walking in muddy **mangrove** forests where sea snakes hang out. Even though it was hot and we got all sweaty, we had a lot of fun. Whenever we found a sea snake, we gently caught it in a special bag made of mesh. Then, we **measured** it, took **pictures**, and even **collected** a tiny piece of its skin to study later. Sometimes it was necessary to bring back a snake to learn more about them in the lab.

Many sea snakes have sharp **fangs** and strong **venom**, so we were super careful not to get bitten. I was amazed by how **graceful**, **peaceful** and **curious** they are when they are swimming in the ocean. One of them even came right up to my diving mask and started checking it out with its tongue! My heart started racing, and I felt both scared and super excited at the same time.

The museum has a wall of sea snakes in jars but there was one we had collected on that trip that I had not seen before. I compared the location where it was found, its head shape, color, size, and scale patterns to other sea snakes and in reference guidebooks. This snake had unique **black and white stripes** and different scale patterns on its head. I also compared the **genetic** information taken from its tissue sample with other sea snake species in the museum's collection and there was no exact **DNA** match. That is when I realized we had discovered a **new species** of sea snake!

unique scale pattern on head

SEA SNAKE

head

jaw

nostrils

black and white colored bands

flattened paddle tail

We gave this new sea snake a **scientific name** so no matter where anyone is around the world, they will know exactly which species it is.

It is important to identify species for conservation because animals may be **disappearing** before we have even realized they exist. The Australian and the Indo-Pacific area are hotspots for sea snake diversity. We did not know much about these animals until recently when marine biologists noticed that numbers of sea snakes were declining. Some sea snakes are eaten but most accidently die when they get caught as **bycatch** in prawn boats.

Later in the day I packed the boat with all our **monitoring** equipment ready for a day out on the **oyster reef**.

# SEA SNAKE FACTS

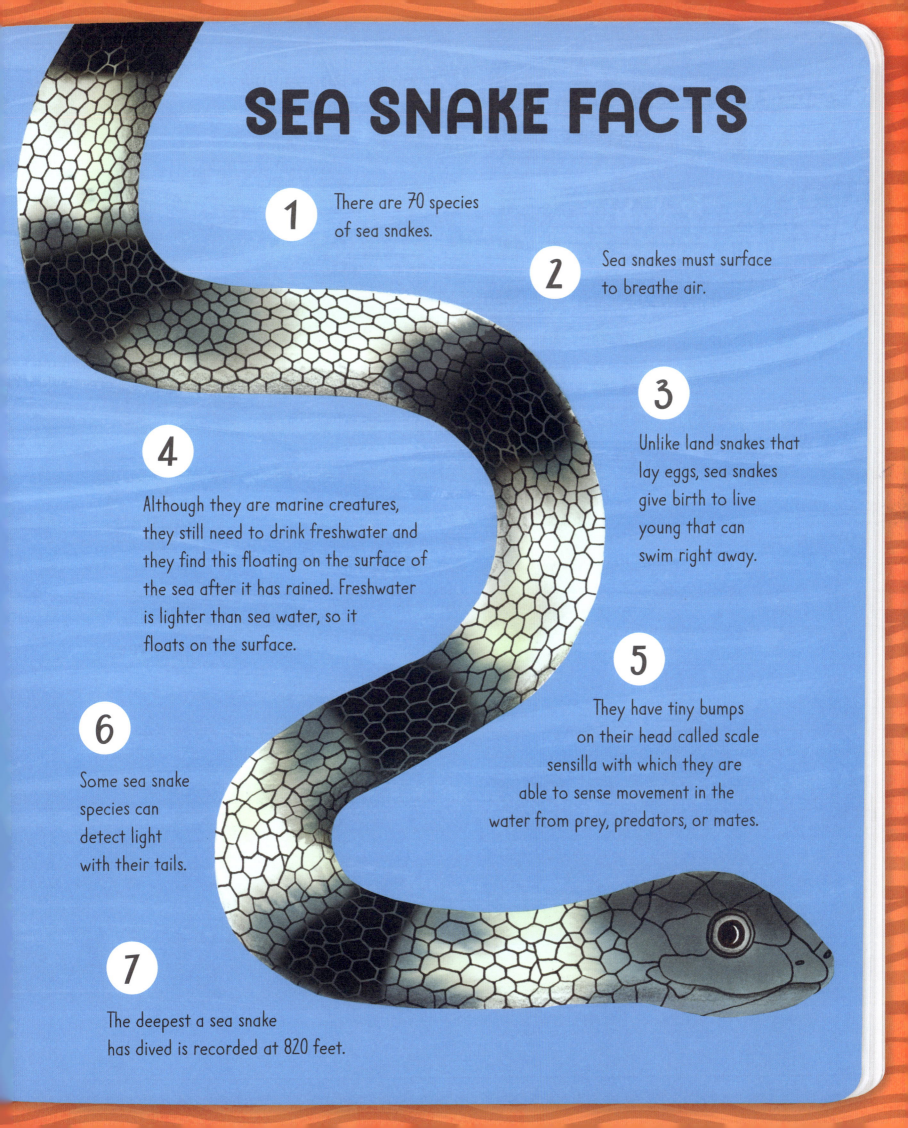

**1** There are 70 species of sea snakes.

**2** Sea snakes must surface to breathe air.

**3** Unlike land snakes that lay eggs, sea snakes give birth to live young that can swim right away.

**4** Although they are marine creatures, they still need to drink freshwater and they find this floating on the surface of the sea after it has rained. Freshwater is lighter than sea water, so it floats on the surface.

**5** They have tiny bumps on their head called scale sensilla with which they are able to sense movement in the water from prey, predators, or mates.

**6** Some sea snake species can detect light with their tails.

**7** The deepest a sea snake has dived is recorded at 820 feet.

# SATURDAY
## LIFE ON AN OYSTER REEF

TIME: _8:00 am_

WEATHER: _25°C Sunny_

LOCATION: _Gulf St Vincent_

Today I dived on a man–made oyster reef. People built the reef to save this **ecosystem** from going **extinct**. It was built by placing thousands of rocks – the size of footballs – and millions of baby oysters onto the seafloor. I was excited to see the restored oyster reef growing. It was covered in a crust of oysters, colorful corals, sponges, and kelp, and fish were swimming among the rocks.

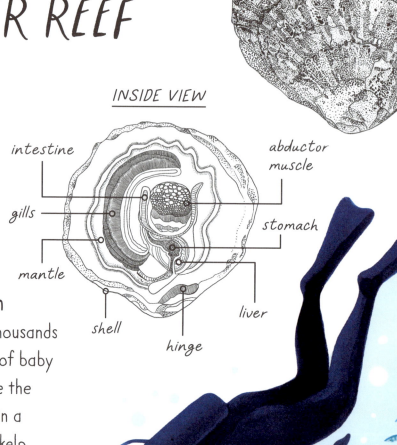

OUTSIDE VIEW

shell

INSIDE VIEW

intestine

abductor muscle

gills

stomach

mantle

liver

shell

hinge

We surveyed the **diversity** of species by rolling a measuring tape out across the reef. We recorded all the marine life we saw: crabs, Snapper fish, a sea urchin, abalone, and a shoal of baby squid. I had to look closely, or I would have missed the octopus hiding in the rocks and the seahorse attached to the seaweed.

Next, we measured how many oysters were living on the reef. I placed a 3 x 3 foot **quadrat** over the reef and counted how many oysters I could see within the square. I counted an average of 200 oysters per quadrat. I collected some oysters to measure their growth. I noticed some oysters were small babies no bigger than a grain of rice and others were adults the size of my palm.

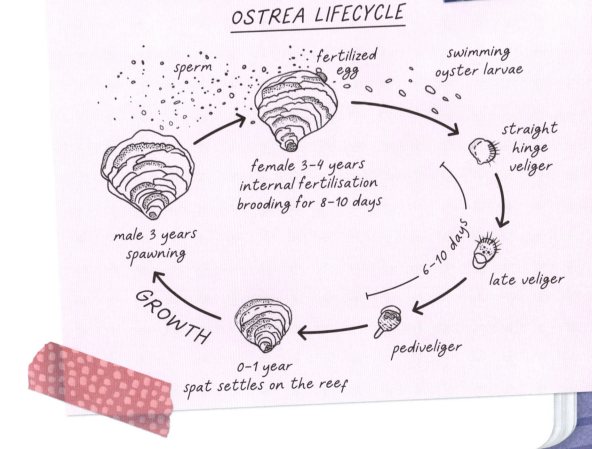

### OSTREA LIFECYCLE

sperm

fertilized egg

swimming oyster larvae

female 3-4 years internal fertilisation brooding for 8-10 days

straight hinge veliger

6-10 days

late veliger

male 3 years spawning

GROWTH

pediveliger

0-1 year spat settles on the reef

It makes me sad thinking that these **temperate** oyster reefs have been lost all over the world. Too many oysters were taken to eat, and the reefs slowly disappeared. Seeing the reef today proved that these reefs can recover if we build them in the right areas.

Scientists are learning how to **restore** oyster reefs as well as other marine ecosystems like seagrass, mangroves, marshes, kelp forests, and coral reefs. It is tricky to restore an ecosystem because they are made up of many **plants** and **animals** that rely on each other to live. Non-living things in the environment like **soil**, **water**, and **air** must also be just right to grow.

Back on the boat we could not stop talking about all the fascinating things we had seen on the reef. We are going to survey the reef again next year so we can compare the changes we see in the **ecology** over time. It is going to take another decade of diving before I see the reef grow to look like a natural oyster reef. I am looking forward to a day off tomorrow and going for a **surf**.

# OYSTER FACTS

SCIENTIFIC NAME: OSTREA ANGASI
SIZE: 4 INCHES

**1** 85% of oyster reefs have been lost globally over the past 150 years.

**2** A football-oval sized oyster reef provides a home to over 100 marine species.

**3** Oysters are the kidneys of the ocean. One adult oyster can filter up to a bathtub of water every two days.

**4** Oysters are hermaphrodites, meaning that they change sex.

**5** Oysters have colorless blood called hemolymph.

**6** When oysters are babies, they can swim, but eventually they settle where they will stay for life.

# SUNDAY
## THE SCIENCE OF SURFING

TIME: _7:00 am_

WEATHER: _25°C Sunny_

LOCATION: _Gulls Rock_

Riding waves makes me feel free like a **dolphin**. When I am **surfing**, I do not have a single care in the world. My best friend Jessica surfs better than me, and she teaches me how to find the best waves and do new tricks.

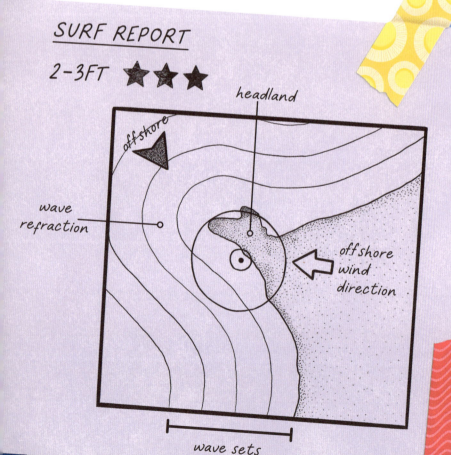

## SURF REPORT

2–3FT ★★★

offshore

headland

wave refraction

offshore wind direction

wave sets

We spent the whole week checking the weather to figure out where to surf. We looked at things like which way the **wind** was blowing, how big the **waves** were, and when the **tide** was coming in or going out. The surf report said the rocky headland would be a great spot today because there would be clean waves, the right wind, the tide going out, and clear skies.

# WAVE REFRACTION

wave slows down at
shallow headland

waves peel off
at side of the
headland

wavesets

headland

beach

beach

# ANATOMY OF A WAVE

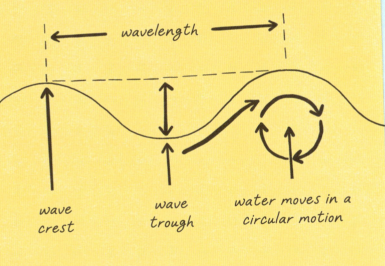

wavelength

wave
crest

wave
trough

water moves in a
circular motion

We paddled out to where the waves were forming. When a good wave came along Jessica turned her board toward the shore and started paddling fast to **match** the **speed** of the wave. I love watching her jump up and get a good ride. It takes practice to read the weather, get balanced, and use your muscles to **paddle** and **steer** on those big, exciting waves. It is a mix of science and fun at the beach!

# PHYSICS OF SURFING

GRAVITY

DRAG

BUOYANCY

We surfed all morning until the wind changed to an onshore direction and the waves became unrideable. As I paddled back to shore, a **seal** popped up near me. It was curious and playful, then swam off to search for food. I saw a plastic shopping bag floating nearby and scooped it out of the water. I was worried that the seal might accidently eat it or get entangled. Thousands of seals, seabirds, sea turtles, and other marine mammals are killed each year from **plastic pollution** in the ocean. It is a big problem that scientists are trying to solve.

Seeing the seal made me realize that surfing means more to me than just catching waves. It helps me to reconnect with nature, calm my mind, and unwind after my busy week. I learn about the ocean even when I am **surfing**, **walking**, **kayaking**, or **fishing**. It is exciting, beautiful, and fragile. Even at times when I have not lived near the ocean I have still dreamt about this big, dark, and mysterious place. There is still so much to discover about the ocean. I will keep **exploring** and **protecting** it, making it better for the future.

# SURFING FACTS

**1**

The water in a wave moves in circles and rises as it rolls to the shore. The bottom of the wave slows down when it hits the seafloor in shallow water, but the top continues to move faster, which causes the wave to curl.

**2**

Surf forecasters use satellite data to track surface winds from outer space to predict where the big surf will be based on oceanic weather patterns.

**3**

The largest wave surfed to date was at Nazare, Portugal and measured 85 feet – the height of a six-story building!

**4**

Most waves are created by winds but a tsunami wave begins far offshore, with an earthquake, volcanic eruption, or landslide.

# BE A MARINE BIOLOGIST:

Watch documentaries, read books, explore websites, and ask questions about the ocean's wonders, and make sure you learn how to swim! The next time you visit the beach, bring a bucket to gather seashells and spend some time exploring rock pools. Observe the birds and fish, count the different types, and discuss their appearances, behaviors, and diets. You can even try using a water quality test kit, volunteer in a citizen science project, or even plan a beach clean-up. Remember, it is never too early (or too late) to start ... and with dedication and love for the ocean, **you too can become a marine biologist.**

# GLOSSARY

*ANEMONE* is an animal with colorful, stinging tentacles that is closely related to coral and jellyfish.

*BLOWHOLE* is a hole at the top of the head through which a whale breathes air.

*BUOYANCY* is what makes things float in water or other liquids, like how a surfboard stays on top of the water.

*BYCATCH* is the accidental capture of fish and other marine creatures trapped by commercial fishing nets.

*CALLOSITIES* are irregular white growths on a whale's head that Southern Right Whales are born with.

*CALVES* is the term for baby whales.

*CHAMELEON* is a lizard that can change the color of its skin.

*CAPTIVE BREEDING* is when wild animals are grown in zoos or aquariums.

*CHROMATOPHORES* are cells in the skin that produce color.

*CITIZEN SCIENCE* is when the public collect information for scientific research.

*CONSERVATION* means taking care of our planet and all the living things on it, like animals and plants, so they can stay healthy and safe for the future.

*DNA* stands for deoxyribonucleic (dee-ok-see-ri-bo-new-klee-ik) acid. It is the genetic information inside the cells of the body that helps make people who they are.

*ECOSYSTEM* is a community of plants and animals that live and interact with each other in the environment.

*EMBRYOS* are unborn animals in the early stages of growth when their basic structures are being formed.

*EXTINCTION* is when every single individual of a particular species or type of animal or plant on earth dies out. Once a species becomes extinct, it is gone forever.

*GENETICS* is the study of how plants' and animals' looks and behaviors pass from one generation to the next.

*GRAVITY* is an invisible force that pulls objects toward the ground.

*HYDROPHONE* is a microphone which detects sound under water.

*LABORATORY* is a place with all the equipment needed for scientists to experiment and watch things closely.

*MATE* is a special friend that an animal chooses to make babies with.

*MONITORING* is to watch and check something carefully in order to discover something about it.

*POD* is the term for a group of whales.

*PHOTOSYNTHESIS* is the process in which plants use sunlight, water, and carbon dioxide gas to make their own food and produce oxygen.

*QUADRATS* are square frames of a set size used to study different habitats such as rocky reefs.

*REFRACTION* is the bending of a wave as it travels at different speeds over different water depths.

*RESTORATION* is recovering an ecosystem that has been degraded, damaged or destroyed.

*TEMPERATE* describes ocean water that isn't too hot or too cold.